$ Profit $ 101

vol. 1

Wesley Jean-Louis

CONTENTS

INTRODUCTION

I will like to first say thank you for purchasing my book. I will then like to congratulate you for taking the first step to making a change in your life. I only ask that you carefully read my book for a better understanding on your journey to becoming successful.

Don't think for a moment that purchasing my book all your problems will be answered without any work being done. Look into the mirror and ask yourself "Do you have the time, energy, and motivation to become a millionaire?" If you can't invest an hour a day of your time, your purchase was a **big mistake** and my book is not for you. You spend about 8 hours a day, five days a week working for some company, so finding an hour out your busy schedule to better yourself should not be a difficult task to accomplish.

I was once facing the same problem you are now facing, (**PROCRASTINATION**). I eventually made the wrong decisions and that cost me my family, friends, and my freedom. I want to help you so that you don't have to ever make excuses or blame anyone for not giving you the chance to make a difference.

TAKE THE FIRST STEP

 W ill you ever achieve anything by running from your problems? The only certain thing you will achieve by running from your problems is <u>losing</u>, getting into more problems and the fact that you will not <u>learn</u> anything by avoiding your problems. You have invested 10 years working for your boss and haven't received a raise. When you take vacations you must cut your vacations short because you're boss needs you back at work and without you the company will not run according to his or her needs. So whose problem is it? Your boss will still have a job, a company to run and if you don't cut your vacation short you will be out of a job. So this will be your problem.

Your first step should be something to fall back on in case of a situation like the one you're in now. If the company you're working for was to close down what would you do? Who would you turn to for help? Whether or not you're in good terms with your boss you must have a backup plan to fall back on, take the step of starting your own small business. (1) Take one day out of the week and put the effort into understanding more about the business world, and how it works.

Over and over you tell yourself you're going to try something different but still you procrastinate or prolong your desire to try something else. Find that courage to take that first step and believe that after doing so you will be a little more confident in your mission. (2) In order to be in your comfort zone you will need a place to work, a place with the least amount of distraction, a place where you know work will get done. If things don't pick up as you planned, don't get frustrated because your ***frustration will oversee your motivation***. Did you know your chances of winning a lottery ticket are 1 out of 40 million? Your chances of starting your own business and being successful are far greater than a lottery ticket or a night out playing bingo. (3) You purchasing my book were your first step away from **PROCRASTINATION**.

Procrastination is a <u>bad habit</u> we all deal with in today's society but you will <u>overcome</u> this habit by <u>blocking out</u> what makes you distracted. It may seem easy said than done, if you continue working on this problem you would have total control of your emotions and bad habits. Now is the perfect time to start a small business. Many investors are holding back due to today's recession and because they are afraid of losing money. If you are afraid of losing money, you will never understand how the business world is run. (4) Map out how you will approach your idea or product into the business world. A weak approach only means you care less whether or not people like or dislikes your <u>project</u>. Take your approach seriously because it may have a big affect that may change your life giving you the chance of not having to deal with someone telling you when or when not to take vacations.

IMPORTANT STEPS TO REMEMBER

1) Find the courage to do something different. When you come up with new ideas make sure to act with caution. What I mean by caution is simply taking your time to plan things out. Don't avoid your problems by turning your back, face your problems so that you may have a better understanding of what causes you to have those problems. Learn from your mistakes don't avoid them.

2) Find a relax place to keep your mind away from distraction. Find your place of comfort where you can call your business office. Remember that being distracted leads to frustration.

3) Find out your bad habits and post them up in bold letters at your business office so that when you're at work you are constantly being reminded of what not to do.

4) Plan out exactly how you will approach your idea. Remember that this is a small business so starting off with a little invested to see how the business world works is

not a bad idea. Learn from any mistakes you may make and you will have a better knowledge of what to look out for the next time.

MONEY

Aren't you sick of hearing," You must invest big in order to make a huge profit"? That is not true. We were all told in school to study so that we could have good grades, so that one day we could become doctors, lawyers, or teachers. We were taught how to add, subtract, multiply, divide, but we were never taught the value of money and how it works. Never were we given the knowledge of money and the true meaning of it. School to me felt like it was only preparing me for a simple life, preparing me to work and pay taxes like generations before me. If you were lucky you were an athlete, actor or a lottery ticket winner. We must teach our kids the true meaning of money and how it works so that one day they could own a company, create jobs and not be living under the middle class standard like the schools are preparing us to.

Aren't you tired of working long hard hours just to be able to pay your bills and have nothing else for yourself? You are afraid of being behind on your bills so treating yourself to something nice is out of the question. When will you say enough is enough? When will you invest into making a difference in your life rather than making someone else's life better than your own? No, I'm not telling you to be greedy or selfish, I'm just telling you to put yourself first for a change. Think about your problems before fixing someone else's.

I believe that life is a gamble. I say this because any decisions you make in life has a good or bad effect on you or someone else. I describe life as a game of monopoly. You have the poor, middle class and the rich. The decisions you make and how you go about using your money will put you in one of these categories. Only you know where you want to be, so get there!

It hurts me to see people suffer because of money. I hate when people say that money isn't everything. You are wrong and I continue to tell my parents this all the time. Its money that puts food on the table, money that keeps the electricity running in your home, money that pays your rent, money that pays the gas in your car, money that pays your doctor if you have any health issues, ect, ect. So I say this for the 100th time "<u>MONEY IS EVEYTHING</u>"!

Can you tell me the <u>secret of money</u>? Well I will tell you what the secret of money means to me. (1) Being able to make more than you spend. (2) Having the knowledge of how money is used. (3) Not having to go and work to make money but <u>having money work for me</u>. This is a technique that our kids haven't learned in school. The skill of making money work for you is a vital skill. When you get to this point you know your well on your way to becoming <u>stress free financially</u>.

It's good to save money for a rainy day but when will you stop saving? Eventually one day it will be raining and you will use everything, then what? Invest a quarter of your savings. If you make a small profit, invest the same amount again before you double down your investment the third time. When you have a better understanding of how your business is run, you can decide how much you can invest.

There are a lot of athletes who are millionaires today, but when they retire have no knowledge of the true meaning of money. They never thought that they would go broke until one day they are left with absolutely nothing. Their house, cars and jewelry is the only thing they have worth any value. They were simply thinking that they were financially stable after retirement. How can you actually believe you are stable financially when there isn't any money coming in? No matter how rich you are today your money will not increase by spending, eventually there will be no money left to spend. I can't understand why they would assure to stay rich without any cash flowing in. So how do you begin a cash flow and how does it work is what you should be asking. Not how do I get rich and <u>not be able to maintain it</u>. Sometimes the answer is in the question. A cash flow is <u>maintaining a steady income</u> every month from other <u>people paying you</u>.

For example, you invested money into property that holds two bedrooms. You're paying the bank $600.00 a month which includes hot water and electricity. You pass on a local ad that you have a two bedroom for rent and that the landlord is willing to <u>negotiate</u>. Start high as $800.00 a month if they take it you are lucky but that's not usually the case. So you got them to take it for $750.00 a month everything included. You just made a profit of $150.00. So imagine if you had 10 or 20 cases like the one you just made a deal on. You now have a <u>cash flow</u> of $1,500 a month or $3,000 a month if you're holding 20 properties similar to the one you first invested on.

There are many ways to invest to make a profit so don't be soo single minded, expand your mind to different ideas with caution. Many young investors rush into certain areas of business without having any knowledge or should I say complete understanding of how a business should run. I urge you to plan out exactly how you tend to approach the consumers interest. There is a great book that I even have in my personal collection called "Rich dad Poor dad", it even comes with a game that gets you ready for the business world.

I never had the chance for someone to educate me about the true value of money. I was always told by my parents that money didn't grow on trees, or why do I need anything more than a roof over my head. I had to often pick at the situation until they eventually caved in and gave me what I wanted. That was a mistake because I did not learn anything about the true value of money. So I guess you can say that I was a spoil little brat. I was heading toward the wrong direction in life, a road that I eventually got lost in and wish I never took. I was hanging out with the wrong crowd of people. My life was no longer in my hands, but in the hands of the street life.

I would hang out late going to parties, strip clubs and gambling was a habit that became an addiction. Everything I had saved up from part time jobs to my personal college funds was all gone. What was I going to tell my parents when it was time to pay for my college courses? I needed to think fast and do something about this issue immediately. A friend of mine told me that I could get a school loan. He told me the maximum loan I can get for each semester was $2,600. I couldn't believe what I was hearing so I went to the school's registration office to apply and was granted $2,600 the first semester. I thought all my problems were finally behind me until it was time to pay the loan back. I didn't have a job so how was I going to return this money back?

How was I going to handle this without my parents finding out? I came up with a plan that got me into a deeper hole, a hole that no ladder can help me out of. I'm too ashamed to talk about it so I'm just going to give you a word of advice. "<u>No bad deed goes un-punished</u>". My point that I'm trying to get across is that not having the proper knowledge of the <u>value of money</u> made me careless and reckless. I was enjoying what the power of money had given me not realizing the trouble it can cause me if not used properly.

IMPORTANT STEPS TO REMEMBER

1) Teach your kids what our generations before was not able to teach us. The power of money and how it should be respected.

2) Before thinking about fixing someone else's problems make sure that you don't have any problems of your own.

3) Don't think for a minute that because you have a lot of money you are rich. If you can't maintain what you have eventually it will be all gone.

4) Figure out how you will start a cash flow. Make sure you have extra investment money until cash starts to flow on a regular basis. Things just don't happen from the snap of your fingers, so always prepare yourself with a back up plan.

ASSETS AND LIABILITY

What is the difference between an asset and liability?

You must know the difference if you want to be a successful investor in the business world.

1) Would you say a car is an asset even if you paid off the loan?

2) Would you say your home is an asset?

3) My brother found a deal on two motorcycles for $2,500 and he rents

them out for $400.00 a week with insurance included. Would you say that be an asset?

4) My father recently paid $3,000 for ten 32inch flat screens and rented them out for $500.00 for each flat screen. The catch is he allowed his buyers to pay $50.00 a month.

5) If everything works out he would cash in a $2,000 profit. What category would my father be in? Would buying flat screens be an Asset/Small Investment/ or Liability?

6) You have bad credit. Your car was taken away due to unpaid car notes and you are asking the back for a loan to put a deposit on a house. What kind of person does the bank see you as?

In order to raise your credit percentage you must start off small as low as $500.00 dollars. When the bank sees that you are a reliable customer your spendable amount will go up. Sooner or later they will be shipping cards to you praying that you take them. Hopefully you have gained at least enough confidence from the bank so that you can now finance a car let's say for $10,000 with $3,000 as a down payment. Take the loan for 2 years so that the bank gets a reasonable interest. Be certain that you have finished paying the remaining balance when the deadline is set. To answer the first question, your car is not an asset because you are not profiting. Yes it takes you from work and back but you are still taking money out your pockets when it comes to buying gas, fixing anything mechanical, to changing the tires. Your car is considered to be a liability due to the fact that you don't know whether or not it will break down on you. Anything that you <u>pay out of your pocket is a liability</u>. Anything someone else <u>pays you on a regular basis is an asset</u>. Your home for example, <u>is not an asset</u> and I'll tell you why. It's only an asset to the bank because the money is going towards the bank not towards your pocket. Your home would only become an asset if you were to rent it out and <u>profit from it</u>. Your home does hold value. Sometimes the value of your home increases. Another way of investment would be re-financing your mortgage. With the money the bank will give you, invest that into an <u>investment property</u>. Another way to make a wise investment would be to take the equity you have from your home. For example, if your home cost you let's say $280,000 and you have already paid the bank $80,000 leaving you with $200,000. You have equity of $80,000. To play it safe you should take one fourth of that and invest it into an investment property. $20,000 will be more than enough in the eyes of the bank as a down payment. I will draw out an example the bank looks for before making any decision.

Figure 1
RICH

Property you own

Investment property

Donate to charity

Figure 2
MIDDLE CLASS

1) They work for someone else.
2) Pay bills on time.
3) Paying mortgage
4) Pay tax
5) Have a little left over to save

Figure 3
POOR

Work to be able to survive. No bank account. No Asset just liability. Pay tax and left with "0".

LOAN=MONEY =LOAN=MONEY

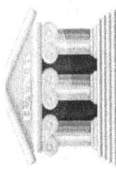

BANK

The bank will continue to loan money to the rich because the rich has assets. Can you tell me why sometimes the rich don't pay as much tax as the poor or middle class? No, it's not because they have all the money and the government is afraid of losing them as customers. They don't pay as much taxes because they show proof of donations to different charity organizations.

SMALL LOAN

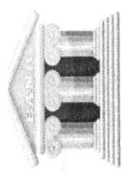

BANK

The bank will loan the middle class, maybe a quarter of their annual salary. If the middle class have a little saved, why don't the banks lend them more money? It's because they don't have any assets. Their home is just a liability. The bank will lend you no more than what you have invested in your home, which is equity.

"CAN'T HELP / SORRY!!"

BANK

Why are the banks turning away from the poor? It is because they are the under-privileged.

You see that's how the banks view people in the world we live in today. What I'm about to give you is some vital information that no bank or real estate agent will ever give you. I sincerely hope with this information given to you that your strive to success is accomplished. In order to get the best deals on property you will need a real estate agent to supply you with information before it gets out to the public. You will tell this agent you need a list of properties that are about to be taken away because the owner can't make payments, any foreclosure or liens. You offer that agent anywhere from $1,000 to $3,000 for that information. Now you have agents working for you and are loyal to you. Money is everything ladies and gentlemen believe me when I tell you that. Everyone should have access to a computer. I will give you a website to go and find information on property with liens. There won't be as much property available but at least it's a start if you are willing to pay some real estate agent for their vital information. Go on taxlien.com and you may find property for a very low cost if agents haven't already taken them. Be careful before purchasing a property. Some properties have enormous amount of damage done to it, which would make it useless to rebuild. Always have someone check out the property before purchasing. You may think at times you have a good deal on a property, it may be worthless and rebuilding the damage alone may cost more than what the property is worth. I know you are wondering what category my father would be placed in from his purchase of the flat screen televisions. The answer is small investment and I will tell you why. My father will no longer own them flat screen televisions after the payments are complete. Meaning he will no longer receive any monthly payments. I believe everyone has the ability to live a fantastic life, dreams can be fulfilled.

My dream as a kid was to be some type of successful businessman. Flying in private jets, traveling the world experiencing what the world has to offer and being with a woman that can relate to the visions I have. Yes life is worth more than working for someone else making them rich. My purpose for wanting to be rich is not so that I can buy and have things I never thought I could have. I wanted to be rich so that I can travel the world helping others understand and realize the true meaning of money and how it works, it's no fun being the only person enjoying the power money has to offer. Don't think for a minute your journey to success will come easy. I hope you're ready to make sacrifices such as your lifestyle. If your way of living requires you to eat at expensive restaurants, dress in fancy clothes and drive in expensive cars your journey to financial success will be a difficult task to accomplish.

IMPORTANT STEPS TO REMEMBER

1) You must know the difference between asset and liability.

2) Credit will play a major part in the business world. Build your credit up from high interest credit cards until your credit score improves.

3) If you're into real estate, find yourself a real estate agent to inform you of what properties with liens are available. Also see taxlien.com

MOTIVATION

I thought life had nothing to offer. Every opportunity that came my way was a failure due to my arrogance. I was lucky to have the opportunity to another chance at success. What I was so ashamed to speak about was being in prison. Everything I got to love disappeared leaving nothing to trace back to. I realize in prison who I really was and being lonely gave me the strength and courage to face life. I was no longer worried about what other people thought or had to say about me. I was now a different man, a man that no longer runs and hides when trouble comes his way, a man that will not take no for an answer, a man who strives for pure love, pure happiness and a man that strives for success.

To all my fans, friends, family and love ones I'm sorry for being a failure in my early stages of life. I only blame myself for the mistakes I made. I know that my mistakes affected others so please forgive me, I'm only human even though I acted like an animal. I was young with a mindless behavior that I have no excuses for. If you are reading my book I know that somewhere inside your heart you forgive me. To everyone that turned their backs on me, thank you because you made me stronger. I would go deeper into my personal life but that is not what my book is really about. If you are feeling guilty about the way you mistreated me, please know that I forgive you. I try to live life with no regrets, sometimes you have one chance to achieve your goals so make the right choices. How do you know what's the right or wrong choice?

Sometimes it's undetectable, but I only can say if it's the wrong choice you will learn from that mistake. I sometimes have bad feelings about certain ideas but I find myself going along doing it anyway. If that happens to you don't think you lost the battle, you just achieved business points for facing your fears.

	1) I can't
	2) NO
ENEMIES:	3) Never
	4) Tired
	5) Stupid
	6) Lazy

These six words are my enemies in the world of business and in life. I battle with at least one of these words every day. These words motivate me to be better at what I do. I refuse to let my enemies defeat me, or allow my enemies to stop me from accomplishing my dreams and my desires to make a difference in my life. Being <u>lazy</u> to make it to a meeting, being called <u>stupid</u> and accepting it, too <u>tired</u> to wake up for work. Telling yourself that you <u>can't</u> do something without even trying and accepting <u>no</u> for an answer is what 70% of the world's population faces every day. I will be that 30%, who will make a difference, be that 30% who will not give up, that will continue to fight for a better life and will continue to help others whether or not I'm successful, that is what makes me different. In order to make a change and move on with your life you must come to the conclusion that something is wrong because if you don't accept that something is wrong you won't think it needs any fixing. Write down what you think needs improvement, ask your family members and close friends to tell you what they dislike about you. Your family members and your close friends should tell you the truth if they have any love for you. Don't blame them for being honest, only thank them for tying to help you make a few changes in your life, changes that were needed in order to move forward. I hope that you are ready for the truth. Some people can't handle the truth begin to blame others for their problems and mistakes. Take every word as an encouragement to motivate you on your journey to success. Words should not hurt you, <u>but encourage you </u>to do better.

My ex-girlfriend was a very nice person and the problem she had was being too nice. People would take advantage of her kindness and I wanted her to change even though I loved her for the person she was. I had a plan that would put our relationship in jeopardy. We would plan to do things together but when that day came I would cancel every time. She would say, "Don't worry baby I understand." I couldn't believe how nice she was, good for me but bad for her. Her birthday was Friday and she took one month planning everything, at the last minute I canceled everything from invitations to her birthday cake. I had seen a side of her I never seen before. She broke up with me that day and didn't call or speak to me for two weeks. She eventually called asking what my problem was and I told her my problems were now fixed. She couldn't understand what I meant by that so I explained. I told her that I was tired of people taking advantage of her kindness and tired of her accepting no for an answer. I told her that I really do love her, but if I had to lose her in order to make her a better person I would.

She then asked me if I was happy. I told her no, no because I miss her and love her more than I ever loved someone before. We eventually got back together and man did I create a monster. She was a different person, a person that I became more attracted to, a person that would not settle for a no or a poor excuse for failure. She became my strength to become stronger and I was hers, not physically but mentally.

My role model is not an actor or professional athlete. My role model is my father and I'm not just saying that to be nice. For a man to come from a country like Haiti with nothing, accomplishing his goals was not going to be easy. He gave me a decent education, shelter over my head, food and clothing. He didn't turn his back on his children when we misbehaved. He encouraged me to make a better man out of myself and I thank him for that. Dad if you are reading my book I want to say thank you for being the man that you are. You were tough at times, but your toughness gave us discipline. Thank you for loving us and loving our mother. I strive for success so that you don't ever have to worry about another days worth of labor. Even the whole time I was in prison you were there to encourage me, give me hope and comfort. I remember you telling me to fill my mind with <u>knowledge</u>. You said that "anything from the neck down was one days hard labor and from the neck up was a "<u>life time's worth of achievement</u>".

For that being said failure is not an option. I'm a winner even when I lose because I will gain knowledge from my mistakes, gain confidence to get back up when I'm down and mental strength to achieve the unthinkable. I refuse to be just an average man with a head on his shoulders, refuse to accept a normal life like generations before me and I refuse to be considered as a middle class person. My strive for success will be accomplished because of my desire to win, desire to be better each day and my desire to be <u>financially happy</u>. Whatever motivates you is what you need to focus on every time you walk into your office. I guarantee you that you will be pushed to work harder, pushed to put in an extra hour into your project.

KEY NOTES TO REMEMBER

1) You don't want to move forward in life with any regrets, having regrets will slow you down and distract you from your project.

2) You must be open minded when it comes to doing business. Concentrating on one direction will leave you blind to what needs to be done.

3) Find what motivates you. Don't ever put your guards down because your enemy will be waiting to interfere with your project. **I can't, no, never, tired, stupid**, and **lazy** is your enemy.

4) Don't push any ideas you may have aside without doing any research on it. Remember it only takes one good idea to start you off your mission to success.

5) Knowledge is priceless, with the things you already know about the business world and about life will help you make your decisions easier. Your mind is the key to overcome your greatest fear, failure.

NETWORKING

Don't be ashamed to rely on help. Networking is an important tool to save you money. The purpose of my book is to make money, maintain your money, help others prosper and have an understanding what the business world is all about.

When I explain my idea to a friend his exact words were "I can't see it." What I seen they could not see because they were using there eyes to spot something that could not be seen and I was working my mind to paint the perfect picture, a picture that needed a road map to get to. Find about 5 people who has the same desires you have, each person has a specific job title and are held accountable for there job. The definition of networking is basically people helping each other, coming with ideas to better your cause. Instead of paying someone to sponsor your idea you will pay less to a network member to advertise your idea for you.

I have a close friend that is a D-Jay. He started off local but now he is global. Everyone wants him to D-Jay at various clubs, private parties, and even weddings. I remember exactly how he started his business. He would give demo tapes away, he would have house parties and be the D-Jay himself. He then started renting out nightclubs and everyone who went to his house parties was now going to his nightclubs. He would make thousands of pamphlets, go from town to town and city to city promoting his talent. Before you know it he was renting out a bigger nightclub to hold a larger capacity. He became popular and famous because of his hard work. It only took time to plan out his vision to become successful. He started doing house parties, free demo tapes, and renting out a nightclub. From one person to the next, the word spread around about his nightclubs and how well he entertained a party.

That's my point ladies and gentlemen, you don't need a whole lot of money to advertise your work or idea. The best advertisement would be word of mouth. Your networking team can be that word of mouth, being in 5 places at once is an impossible task doing it alone but with a networking team it is a piece of cake.

Did you know that if you start saving $500.00 a week from the age of 21 you would be a millionaire when you are in your sixties? Most people retire around the age of 65 so if you are in your 20's that is something to think about. But for me being a millionaire in my sixties is not part of my goals. I'm working on being a millionaire now. So that when I get to my 40's I can be around more in my children's life. What works for me may not work for you. Be your own person, be comfortable with what works for you and not what did work for someone else. Be a part of something new and be different. People will love you for being yourself not for acting to be something you are not because they will see right through you. Always be honest with your networking team. Any disloyalty only would mean no control, without any control you will have chaos. Think of the business world exactly like this: The ones with the business have the money, the ones with the money have the power and the ones with power have <u>total control</u>.

A friend of mine who I became really social with once said to me, "Why spend 10, 20, 30 minutes or even an hour of your day with people that have no clue what goals they want to achieve in life?" I said, "To help them understand my purpose, my mission to success and that there is opportunities for them out there." He laughed at me. He said "In order to have anyone believe in your mission to success, you must first achieve it" He had a point, but I was not going to let that discourage me. My mind was already set and there was no turning back. Everything was planned out exactly how I visualized it in my mind. My project was not going to start off easy but eventually everything will fall into place. I had a team of networkers placed in Canada, Atlanta Georgia, Florida and in New York. Advertisement is not easy to come by so all of my faith went to my team of networkers. I also used Face Book as an advertisement tool. They are over five million people logging in and out of Face Book. I used Face Book as a form of business instead of using it as a social media. My ex-girlfriend told me about Face Book years ago and I laughed at her, telling her that Face Book was for kids that had nothing else to do with there life. If you are reading my book I would like to apologize for talking to you with such disrespect. You were right, Face Book is a useful tool for advertisement. I thank you for being who you are and never changing.

In the early chapters of my book I said that life was a gamble. If you're going to make a decision in your life, don't gamble with your life doing a crime. Whether or not you were caught, don't forget that no bad deed goes un-punished. I thought I was untouchable and that the law was for everyone else to obey but me. I was wrong and I came to the conclusion that even the lawmakers must respect and live according to the law. If you are going to achieve your goals you must not try taking any shortcuts. What will you learn from avoiding taking your time? You might miss vital information that could have been the answer you were looking for. Respect the plan you have set out for your mission to financial success.

What do you think that someone who wanted to be a professional basketball player do to achieve his or her goal? My guess would be to practice 3 to 4 hours a day shooting the basketball, running 4 to 6 miles a day and playing with other basketball players better than they are to have a better knowledge of the game. My point is to find ways to prepare your mind for challenges. Read entrepreneur magazines, which is the number 1 business magazine there is. Entrepreneur is another way you could advertise your product, go to Entrepreneur.com. You can also start your own website to advertise your project, go to godaddy.com to begin your own website. I believe that everyone already knows about E-bay, go to E-bay.com to advertise your product. Once you log in on one of these websites you will be directed on how to start your own website. You don't need to be someone with a college degree to follow simple directions.

The average person will continue working on a project over and over again even if they are losing money. If you are not gaining a profit after putting the time in to achieving your goal, it's time to call it quits!!! Your budget can only handle so much, how far are you willing to go to understand that you are in deficit and that you are hurting yourself if you continue?

If you have read the early chapters of my book it tells you to work according to your <u>budget</u> and to <u>respect your plan.</u> You have not only wasted money, you have also wasted time for a lost cause. Just because your idea or product wasn't a success doesn't mean you are a failure. Your idea was probably good but your approach was terrible. Maybe your team of networkers did not take your mission serious, maybe the economy was just not ready for your idea, or maybe your place of advertisement needs to be rearranged. This world has many countries, many states, many cities and towns that may love your idea. Try advertising somewhere else to see what happens before forgetting about the whole idea.

IMPORTANT STEPS TO REMEMBER

1) People helping other people. Start up your networking team to save you money. Your networking team should have the same desire for success as you. Choose your team wisely.

2) You should also advertise your idea or project with Face Book. You have over 200 Face Book friends, so use that to your advantage (people helping people).

3) You can log onto E-Bay.com, Entrepreneur.com, to start advertising or you can start your own website at godaddy.com.

4) I urge you to continue to exercise your mind so that you can handle any challenges that come in your path to success. Read business books such as "Rich dad Poor dad" and entrepreneur magazines to motivate your desires.

ECONOMY

In today's economy we are facing a shortage in jobs, high prices in oil and the government as well is in deficit. How do we pay bills or put food on the table if our hours at work decrease? Why is our economy struggling and suffering? Where is all of our money going and how is our money being used? How do you explain to someone that they would have to find another home because they were not able to pay their mortgage on time due to this recession? Do you think people will trust the government again? Those who were making $70,000 a year have to now settle for $40,000. Banks are not giving many loans out if any. People are not shopping and taking vacations like they use to. When will we get answers instead of promises? Why is it that no one is being held accountable for this recession? The rich is getting richer, and the middles class, as well as the poor is suffering. Is that how life is suppose to treat innocent human beings? When will the economy receive the help they need before people are forced into the streets? It's hard for me to say this but life goes on and that's the truth.

If this economy that we live in doesn't fit your standard of living you must take action. You must do what's necessary for you and your family. Do your research, find out how you and your family can survive somewhere else. United States is not the only country you can make a living. Like I said before don't be so single minded, expand your mind. Example, the cost of living in Canada is cheaper than the cost of living in United States. Canada also has a free health care plan. This may be a hard decision to make but you must think about your future and your family. Remember that great opportunities are not <u>seen with your eyes they are seen with your mind.</u> I really love the United States with all my heart, but when it comes to my survival and my family I will make that difficult decision to move on.

For the rich, they are taking advantage of this recession. They are buying homes that have liens on them, homes with foreclosure, investing in stock and buying businesses from owners that are too afraid to maintain it. The rich believe that the economy will get better in the near future and that investing now is a great decision for them, buying everything is not a bad idea if you're <u>rich and patient</u>. But if you're living under the middle class bracket taking a chance like that is very risky for your budget. If you are living under the poor class you should not make any risky decisions for the next five to ten years if you're lucky. Don't believe for a second that because you are down you will not be able to get back up. Life is full of surprises and opportunities for you. My strength was my faith. My faith to succeed, to overcome fears, to fight using my mind and not to take no for an answer was what I used as a road map to success. Encourage yourself because no one else will.

I would say my brother Pierre is a very wise man. He was someone that loved to live the life of a millionaire. He would drive in expensive cars, eat at expensive restaurants and dress from head to toe in style. As soon as the recession began he sold his BMW, his $220,000 dollar home, rented out an apartment and stopped eating at expensive restaurants. Since he was always on the road delivering merchandise from state to state he really did not need to buy a home. I really look up to him because he made heart-breaking decisions that most people would not think of making. He said that until the economy improves he will not spend any money if it wasn't necessary. For someone to be living the life of luxury, decisions like the ones my brother made don't come easy. The problem that most people in this economy have is waiting for miracles. I will say that it is true," Good things happen to those that wait", but those who wait have choices. If you are struggling to pay your bills on time or struggling to find that extra cash, you don't have choices, you have problems. Don't think that money will fall from the sky to your lap, don't think that you can sleep your problems away or think that the government will erase all your debt and pay all your bills for you.

Let's say that would all happen, what would you learn from someone always taking care of all your problems? What will you do to avoid that from ever happening again? Why would anyone lend you money if you don't have any plan or financial intelligence whatsoever? A person with no goals has no motivation for anything positive. Try showing at least a little effort fixing your problems. Avoid whatever it is that's influences you to negativity, there is so many things you can do with your spare time but you rather wait for your problems to go away. How much in debt will you go into until you realize what you're doing simply does not work? The president of the United States recently raised the level of debt, no disrespect Mr. President but if we cannot seem to get ourselves out of the first debt we are in, what makes you think we can handle a greater amount of debt? What this country needs is more entrepreneurs and more jobs. Giving money to someone without them having any plans whatsoever is meaningless!!! It helps for the moment but when it's gone then what? Who will they turn to then? Who do you think they will blame?

Raising the taxes on corporations did not do us any good as well because they turned around and raised their prices. So we are not only suffering financially, we are finding it difficult to put food on the table, gas in our cars and clothes on our children. My point is that allowing the middle class and poor class people to live comfortable accepting government funding would only hurt them in the future. If we don't create more jobs they will rely on more government funding, if they are given more government funding this economy will be in more debt. The government will tax business owners and corporations will only raise their prices. Who will hurt more when this happens? The MIDDLE CLASS and the POOR!!!

Success is not promising but at least it beats suffering from an economy crisis. You have the power and knowledge to do something about your financial problem. All you need is time, time to plan and put that effort into your goal. Your goals will be met as long as you put the work into it. If I offend anyone, I apologize. I don't mean to, I'm only trying to encourage you to do your best. Don't blame or point fingers at anyone but yourself. Don't wait around, make the change to better yourself and your family. Do what it takes to survive this crisis. Yes, this is a crisis because your home, your health and family are suffering. No one will help you if you can't help yourself. How long do you expect to survive this recession if you're not doing anything about it? Be a man/woman, be someone for your kids to look up to, be that role model, that person to make a difference so that others could follow. Push yourself, give it all you have, don't be a quitter and don't ask yourself if you can. You will get things done, you will survive this recession, and you will pay your bills and put food on your table.

I wrote this book because I love you. I hate to see people struggle. You're my family whether you are black, white, green and red. We must help each other, encourage each other to be able to survive. I believe in you, all that was needed was a hand to get up from the floor, now you're able to walk this journey alone. You are ready to face your fears, ready to take a stand for what you want, for what you desire.

IMPORTANT STEPS TO REMEMBER

1) Don't sit around waiting for someone else to fix your problem. Everyone is not accountable for your personal problems.

2) If you are struggle financially make that difficult decision finding somewhere else to make a difference in your life. Your problems will affect your family, so fix it before it gets to that point.

3) What will you learn from someone else fixing your problems? The answer is nothing. Learn from your errors, don't adapt to someone helping you.

4) If you have extra money lying around now is the time to invest in real estate while the prices are low. Sooner or later things will start picking up from where they were left off, invest cautiously.

5) The rich take chances because they are not afraid to lose and the fact that they are patient when it comes to investing!

SMALL BUSINESSES

It really doesn't take much to start your own small business. A teenager could start a small business, so why can't you? People think that the need for a large amount of money is the only way to start a business. They are wrong, that's why it's called a small business. A demand on your store supplies may not be a high impact right away. Be patient, see what it is that attracts the consumers attention. It could be the color, the size or even the name of your product. Details can make a big difference when it comes to business. The way you talk to consumers, dress and how you make an approach. Make a good approach, address your product clearly so that there is no misunderstanding.

Practice on your disadvantages, meaning working on whatever it is to make your business grow.

The advantage that I have is being very social. Being able to listen, answer questions and make people comfortable as if they knew me very well. Your attitude is important when it comes to running a business. Stay positive and relax at all times so that you do not frighten your customers. If you give your customers the service they need, not only will they come back, they will <u>advertise your business to others.</u> In the beginning your business will only be a liability because you will be spending money to maintain it, advertise it and pay workers if needed. Imagine the feeling of being in control, the feeling of being financially stable, and the feeling of not answering to any boss telling you what to do. Right now all you can do is imagine until you make it into reality. Make your dreams come true, make the impossible possible so that you can live a fantastic life. The only person that can stop you from accomplishing your task is yourself. You are in total control, you are the one who set these goals so there are your rules, your plan that must be followed in order to succeed.

My father came to this country with $300.00 in his wallet. His dream, his desire to be successful was not an easy task, but for the love of his family he would not give up, he started as a delivery man supplying local schools with fresh baked bagels. After five years he had enough money saved to open up his own business. He had the knowledge he needed to open his own business after working for someone else's company. He decided to open up his own bagel shop. He already had clients from small diner owners and county prisons. His plan was to give all his client's contract deals so that they wouldn't look anywhere else. After two years the demand for his bagels grew. On the weekends my brother and I would work with my dad to have a better understanding of how the business world works. I didn't do it for the money, I did it for the knowledge the fact that I have a lot of love and respect for my father. At the time I was only 16 years old with the knowledge of a business man that have been running a company for decades. I know I was going to run my own business one day. I knew that was the reason why my father always wanted me to be around him and his company. He turned me into a walking business machine.

At the age of 18 I found the deal my father had been waiting for. A local pizza store that I have been going to since I was 8 years old was growing and the owner wanted to invest his wealth into something promising. I told him about my father's small bagel shop and how it has been growing to the point where he needed to hire workers. The pizza owner asked me if my father wanted to sale his bagel shop to let him know. That night I asked my father how much would he sale his shop for if he wanted to? My father said he only invested $30,000 for his bagel shop and that it's hard to say. He paused for a minute as if he was thinking of a figure and said $65,000. My father then said when you invest you always want to at least double your money back. One week later I ran into the pizza store and the first thing that came out the owner's mouth was how much? The first thing that came out my mouth was $120,000. He asked me why so high? I told him that the bagel shop is growing and there is a big demand to the point where my dad needs to hire workers. I then told him that my father would also give him the list of clients that he had.

The pizza owner wanted to take a look at my father's bagel shop and if it was to his expectations he would agree on the $120,000 deal. After looking at my father's bagel shop the deal was a go. I went home instantly to tell my father the news. My father was in disbelief. I showed him the paper work and told him the pizza owner wanted to finalize everything as soon as possible. My father then said, "If everything is what you say it is you can have half the take," I said no dad, you already gave me what I needed. You gave me the knowledge to run my own business one day, save the money dad in case of an emergency or to invest into something else.

I was given the knowledge of how to buy, sell and the knowledge of how to make a customer comfortable to the point where they feel as if they knew me for a long time. Not anyone can make the deal I made at such a young age. My dad was impressed by me making that deal. He was able to give the bank back there $30,000 and have $90,000 left to do as he wish. My father started investing in real estate, the banks were happy to loan my dad money to invest due to the last payment that he paid. I started learning different aspects of investing.

Don't think that just because you have a small business it will not pay off. The time and work that you put in will determine how your business will do. My father was now buying homes at low cost and renting them out. In two years he will have the $70,000 he invested back in his pocket. The $20,000 that was left was there as backup in case something needed to be fixed, bought, built, etc. In five years my father would have tripled his money and some. My father did not graduate from high school or took any business courses. He took chances rather than sitting around and waiting for money to fall from the sky!!! The opportunities are out there waiting for you, make that first move off the couch, that bed, and reach for your goal to become financially stable. Whether or not my father was successful he would always be my role model because he took a chance at success, he made things happen rather waiting for the government to give him <u>handouts</u>!!!

Real estate is not the only thing you can do for a profit. You can get into the export and import field. The world is open up for business ladies and gentlemen. Be your own boss, make your own decisions and create your own working hours. I have a friend who imports clothing from China and are being sold in

Canada. For example, the price for a pair of Timberland Boots in Canada are anywhere from $170.00 to $220.00. The price he pays for them in China are anywhere from $10.00 to $20.00 depending on the quantity. That is just an idea for you to think about. Try looking into Nikewholesale.com or Chinawarehouse.com, do your research on the market, find out where your business could be useful before getting involved. Find out the tax rate for importing and exporting to determine what price you would set your merchandise.

Winter coats would cost more in places like Alaska, Canada and would make you a sizeable profit then places like Florida, California or Texas. Pin point where there would be a demand on certain merchandise. Don't just get involved in business and be clueless of what to do. Most small companies, last for about 2 or 3 years. Did you know that if you maintain your company and show proof of substantial profit you could be eligible for a loan depending on your <u>net worth</u>? Any bank in this country would approve a loan to you if you can maintain your small business for 2 to 3 years. Banks are not just available for deposits and withdrawing money. Your money is being invested as soon as it is deposited in the bank to someone with knowledge of what to do with it. Be that someone, take charge because who knows what the outcome would be if you don't do anything to move forward. You will either be in the same place you were or be way back behind to even catch up to pay your bills on time.

IMPORTANT STEPS TO REMEMBER

1) Work on your approach so that your consumer will have a better understanding.

2) Know your customers, understand what they want or need to make your customers comfortable, relax at all times is important for your business. You do want your customers happy, **right**?

3) Giving your customers the service needed will increase your supply and demand.

4) Don't just be single minded to one area for advertising your business. Expand your business to <u>different areas</u>.

MY EXPERIENCES

I was always a smart young man that only needed guidance while pursuing my goals. Not that I could not handle myself but only to assure that I would not get carried away with my work.

It was the summer of 2003 when I decided I would no longer ask anyone for help or advice. I needed to make some money without asking my parents. I had only $15,000 dollars to my name, which was nowhere near what I needed to invest. I wanted to start promoting and Canada was the perfect place to do so. I was told that it would cost me $10,000 as a deposit fee alone to book any up and coming artist.

It would cost me $ 7,500 to rent out a place that can hold a capacity of 600 people. I was too afraid to invest the only money I had left. I was only living in Canada for 7 months and did not know the area well or the language. It was impossible for me to get a better deal due to the fact I was from another country trying to invest my American dollars.

My cousin who has never worked a day in his life offered to help me invest my money. He offered to give me $22,000 if I was able to loan him my $12,000 for 3 months. When I asked him how he was going to profit from my money he replied, "It's better left a mystery." With that being said I already know what his plans were, whatever it was I'm sure it was not <u>legal</u>. Without giving this situation a second thought I gave him the money. I was tired of procrastinating and asking my parents for help. Do remember I was facing imprisonment for selling drugs in the United States, so being involved with any illegal activities was not in my mind whatsoever. On the 3rd month my cousin handed me $22,000 dollars. I know it may not seem like a lot of money, but for someone that could not get a job due to my past, it was more than enough.

Now was the time to invest the money I had to do the right thing. After three weeks of trying to find the perfect deal I realized that my chances of being a promoter were slim. I was either told that the artist I wanted would not travel to Canada for less than $40,000 or told that the artist had prior felonies which would not allow them to cross into Canada. No matter what I did it was not working for me. How was I going to maintain $22,000 without a job or any goals? Certain family members were hounding me due to the fact they knew that I had $22,000. How could I tell them no I can't lend them any money knowing that I have it and the fact that they are allowing me to stay in there home which is considered to be harboring a fugitive. I did not lend them the money because I wanted to be nice. I lend them that money in fear if I didn't they would call the police.

After lending out most of what I had left me with $10,000 dollars. I knew at that point I had to leave and find a new place to call home. Without any Canadian papers who would rent me an apartment? Who would sign the lease for that apartment trusting that nothing would go wrong? I came up with the plan to use my money wisely so that no questions like the ones I just mentioned would be asked. I found a two-bedroom apartment renting out for $500.00 a month. I offered the landlord $3,000 which covers the rent for 6 months, he agreed. I was now left with $7,000 to my name. By the time I got finished with furniture, clothes and food I was left with $4,000. I was now in a deeper hole, I totally disregarded <u>the value of money</u>. I was now going backwards. I needed to get something going so I could survive for the next six months.

The next day my cousin called me and asked me, if I wanted to buy the new play- station game that recently came out. I asked him for a price and he said that the guy was looking for a gram of cocaine. I said, "Where the hell would I get that from?" My cousin laughed, and said well give me $50.00 dollars and I will get you the play station. I said "What"? For something worth $400.00 dollars don't you think $50.00 dollars is way too cheap? My cousin told me not to worry about that, its business. When I received that play station it was in excellent condition, straight out the box. I asked my cousin if he was able to get anymore and he said as many as I would like. For something I can only pay $50.00 for and sell back for at least $250.00 was going to be a good investment. I asked my cousin to get me 80 play stations for the total of $4,000. I was taking the chance of investing my last dollar to make $16,000.

What kid in their right mind wouldn't take a deal like that, charging everyone $250.00 would save them $150.00. I also gave them a 30-day money guarantee. They would hand me the extra $30.00 and if something happened to that play station before 30 days I would exchange it for them. So on top of the $16,000 I was getting an additional $2,400 giving me a total of $18,400. Wow, I was amazed at myself for the way I pulled that together within two months. At that point I knew for a fact I had the will and the intelligence to achieve my goal if I wanted to.

Before I continued I would like to say that I was wrong for the crime I committed in the past and that everyday I regret the decisions I made. I did not only hurt myself, I hurt my family, friends and the women I thought I was going to live with for the rest of my life. I made mistakes like any other human being but at least I can admit I was wrong and apologize for it. If

I was able to go back in time and change the bad decisions I made, I would so that no one would be hurt by my actions. All I can do as of now is live righteously hoping that the people I had hurt in the past would forgive me. I was young and careless living life one day at a time with no plans or goals. Like I said in the earlier chapters of this book," **no motivation equals to no goals**". I see life totally different when you have goals to achieve. Keeping myself busy at all times kept me away from negativity.

Doing what was wrong was easier to do than doing what was right. Losing everything from material things to love ones was something I never wanted to experience again. I lost my friend Wesler who died from a violent act. That person who committed this heartbreaking act was never apprehended. I'm not even sure if the police have any leads. Wesler was more than just a friend to me, he was like my brother, someone that I can trust, talk to and count on for anything. He was the type of person who you can talk to for advice. We were alike in some ways, which makes perfect sense why we were so close. I blame myself at times for his death because I know for a fact if I was there this terrible act would not have taken place. In the business he was in, he should have never been hanging out in some town he was not from. That was the careless decisions he would make while I was away at prison. What he did for money was not righteous but that does not say what kind of person he was.

My point to this chapter is to make it easier for you to choose from doing the right or wrong things with your life. Take me as an example that doing the wrong things to gain money is not the way to go. I have to do 6 years in prison before I could get deported to Haiti. A country that I could hardly remember being from, a country with humanitarian problems. That will not stop me from succeeding, from making a difference or doing something positive. It doesn't matter where you're from or at in this world, you work hard to achieve your goals you will succeed. Don't allow your problems to make it hard for you or allow you to give up on your dreams. Believe in yourself, believe that nothing can come between your strive to become financially happy. As we get older our faith and beliefs fade away. Recapture what the heart and mind allowed to slip away from you. Don't be ashamed to believe in something you can't see with your eyes. You do know that there is a greater power that created us? A greater power known to mankind as GOD.

God can't be seen with your eyes, but your heart believes in God. Well, that's how I see my work, my goals and my desires to become financially happy. I can't see all the million of dollars and big mansions I want, not yet of coarse but I believe I will achieve that goal. Only person that can disappoint you is yourself, only person that can tell you that your goals are unachievable is yourself.

I don't feel sorry for myself, actually I feel bless to experience the things I have experienced. I know how it feels to have absolutely nothing, how it feels to have family and friends betray you for money. When I had money I was loved by people I did not even know, greeted by people I never seen before in my life and women would ask me to sleep with them even if it was for one night. I had too much respect for myself, too much to risk sleeping with someone I knew nothing about. I was carrying my family's last name so I would not disrespect my family's image. My parents always said I would know who my true friends were if I was in trouble. Oh man was my parents right. I couldn't believe my girlfriend who I thought was the love of my life leave me and friends who I thought I could count on leave me as well since I went to prison. The difference with me is that I forgive them for turning their backs on me, life is too short to have any grudges or hate in my heart.

I did this to myself, I put myself in this situation no one else did so I will handle it like a man even if I must handle it alone. I was hurt at the time, feeling betrayed, lonely and mistreated but I came to the conclusion that "what doesn't kill me will make me stronger"! I will survive, I am stronger mentally and physically. All I needed was time to realize who I was and what I wanted to accomplish in my life. Prison was a gift from God, prison was my reward. I know you're wondering about what I meant by my previous statement, that prison was a gift or reward. I never had time to myself, never had the space I needed to know who I was and what I wanted. Being in prison I finally was at peace with the world. I didn't have to worry about satisfying anyone to like me, did not have to be depended on or worry about making someone else happy. I don't mean to disrespect anyone that knew me but I was feeling smothered, feeling like I was doing all the thinking and all of the planning for achievements. Now I will live my life instead of helping someone live his or hers.

I would first help myself before trying to help others. If I'm stuck in a hole and you're stuck in a hole how is it possible to help one another? I have nothing but love in my heart for everyone and I pray that you all achieve your goals. You can live the life that you dreamed about. I know it sounds easier said than done. Nothing in life is promising but getting old and death. What do you really have to lose trying to achieve your goals? Are you afraid of failure? Are you afraid of being rejected? Why wouldn't you want to show the world what you're made of? If you have talents why not share it? My talent was the ability to make something out of nothing and the ability to turn $1.00 dollar into a $100.00 dollars. That's why my friends call me Profit. I live by the phrase <u>"If it's not worth it, I don't touch it"</u>! If you have an idea you know that you will profit from, why not invest? Well write me and I'll take a look at it. Even if it means I have to invest a dime to make a quarter I'm all for it, <u>money is money no matter the value.</u>

If you had a million quarters how much money do you have? I'm sorry the answer is still a million quarters but how much would that be translated to dollars? You must know the true value of money even if that means pennies, nickels, dimes, and quarters. The answer to my question is two hundred and fifty thousand ($250,000). It's never too late to understand the value of money, you're never too old to get involved with investing.

Recently I was reading an article about a man who was recycling cans as a hobby. In 4 years he made a million dollars off cans alone. He would have to collect 5 million cans a year to make $1 million dollars in 4 years. Each can is worth 5 cents and 5 million cans is worth $250,000 <u>X</u> 4 years which equals to $1 million dollars. Open your mind for ideas such as this one. People are throwing away money everyday without realizing it. People are worried about making that huge profit without realizing the little things. This man did not care about what people thought about him. Who dares to laugh at a person that made a million dollars even if he made it collecting cans? I salute that man, I look up to that man for not allowing anyone or anything to get in the way of his pursuit to a million dollars. Usually the smallest things are never spotted when it comes to investing. Don't worry about the time it would take to make a million dollars if you're profiting from whatever it is your doing.

Your mission is to make money and not waste time with your idea if you're losing money. If your idea simple doesn't work you should forget about investing your money before losing everything you have. I believe that you are intelligent enough to know when something simple doesn't work to quit. Quitting doesn't mean you're a loser, it doesn't mean you can't finish what you started or doesn't mean you are not ready to run a business. Running a business is not a piece of cake so don't feel bad when your business is not running as you planned, bailing out is not always a bad idea. I was always the type to allow my pride to get control of my decision-making. I was concerned about how my friends would look at me, concerned about having no time for myself and I was finding it difficult to take orders from anyone but my parents. Being able to take orders or follow simple instructions is only a small task. Instead of having an attitude, I should have swallowed my pride and taken advantage of what I was being taught.

That is one of the problems that young people in this society deals with everyday. Either they are too stubborn or think that they know it all. If I would of taken my parents advise when I was in my early 20's, I believe I would never had experience prison. Since I'm a strong believer of the statement that "everything happens for a reason", I'm totally okay with how my life turned out. People do look at you differently after knowing that you have been in prison, the important thing to remember is how do you look at yourself? What will you do with your life from this day on? You can still achieve your goals even if prison played a part of your life. The government has loans and grants available for people coming out of prison. You may find this information at any <u>city hall</u> located in your state. Don't think for a second that it's over for you because you went to prison. You can still chase your dream if you stay motivated and confident.

I want you to make sure that when you do succeed not to forget about the hard work you put in to get there and not to forget about the people that helped you get there. Once you are at the level you need to be, you can help others get out of that hole you were once in. People helping people remember? That is the point you must put across while helping the next person. What fun is there having all the money and not share? I guess that's the type of man I am, a man that wants everyone to live the life they always dreamed about, the life of not having to worry about how I will pay my bills, buy my wife a decent birthday gift or how will I find the time and money to go on vacations.

We all would love to experience doing all of these things but that will not happen waiting and hoping that money falls from the sky. If you're reading this book I believe you are trying to make a difference in your life, that you're sick and tired of waiting for a miracle and that you will make <u>changes</u>. If you're doing the same things over and over again without getting any good results, yes change is good.

KEY NOTES TO REMEMBER

1) Live righteously, remember that no bad deed goes unpunished. Treat people the way you would love to be treated.

2) Don't allow your pride to get in the way of your mission to succeed. Do not worry about what people have to say or think about you.

3) You only live once so don't leave anything behind, meaning give it your everything. No one can stop you from succeeding but you.

4) Before trying to help someone else you must help yourself first. Two people stuck in a hole can't help one another.

LIFE

A) We are role models, role models that our children look up to. What kind of example will you set for your children? They see you work almost every day just to put food on the table, just to come home from work being tired for any other activities. At what point will you and your family be able to enjoy life?

B) Budget: You must set a reasonable budget so that you don't be in deficit. Respect your <u>spending strategy</u>, increase your <u>savings technique,</u> and create a format for paying your bills. It's not always a good idea to pay the complete balance on your bill. It would be wise to pay at least 40% of your bills so that you can be left with something to save. As long as you're paying something for your bills you will not have any problems. They want you as a customer, believe me when I tell you that.

C) Credit: Your credit is poor. In my early chapters I speak about taking high interest credit cards until your credit improves. Charging everything you purchase on your credit card is a great way to improve your <u>credit score</u>. It's not a wise idea to pay anything cash if you are holding a credit card. Take <u>advantage</u> of what the banks have to offer. Your credit will determine what <u>loans</u> you can or cannot be approved for. I remember when I was 19 years old trying to finance my first car. I was told that I had to place a certain amount of money as a down payment in order to get approved for the remaining balance. If my credit score wasn't so bad the car dealer would not have needed any money as a down payment. It's not the fact that my credit score was bad, the problem was I did not have any credit to take control of my life without depending on anyone to help me. I was wrong for doing so. I should have allowed my parents to help me. If I was to allow my parents to <u>co-sign</u> for me I would have saved money. The bank would have seen my parents with a perfect credit score which would have saved me that down payment and a <u>lower interest rate</u>. Allowing my parents as the co-signer would of increase my credit score just as well. Sometimes as young adults we tend to do things without thinking. I urge you to stop and think about whatever it is before making that final decision. Mistakes can be avoided if you take the time to <u>think it through</u>.

D) Doubt: When it comes to making final decisions there should be no doubts that everything is going according to plan. If you're <u>not comfortable</u> with a certain idea why go along with it? Why put the effort, time and money doing something that you're not sure about? I had doubts in life and I ended up doing it anyway because I was a stubborn individual, a risk taker and someone that did not listen to advice whether it was good or bad. I ended up in prison, a place that I would never wish upon someone. Take my advice, if you're feeling doubtful about any situations don't get involved. You're not a coward, not a loser or a quitter, you're intelligent for not going forward with something you don't feel comfortable with.

E) Courage: To leave my family at such a young age to chase my dreams was not easy. I was afraid of leaving the place I called home, the place I got too comfortable with, the only place I knew I could be myself. I had to make that decision even if I knew I would be home sick. It was time for me to be a man and start dealing with responsibility. That day I believe I was courageous, making that decision to leave home to take on responsibility. Face your fears, believe in yourself because no one else can convince you but yourself. If you tell yourself you can achieve your goals it will happen.

F) Marketing: What effective strategy will you use to advertise your merchandise? Banks will feel comfortable working with established companies which can be accomplished by providing the bank materials such as newspaper ads, flyers or even magazine ads. Providing the bank with your plan on how you will attract customers and how you will make a reasonable profit will help your chances.

G) First Employee: When it comes to hiring your first employee you must be sure that this person will help your business improve. Hiring the wrong person will result in wasted time and thousands of dollars lost. You must acknowledge which employee would be best for your company. You will know when it's time to hire another employee after receiving the proper service from the first one. Don't just hire anyone because the demand of your business is needed or simple because you need the help. It only takes one bad employee to ruin everything you worked so hard for. Don't make that mistake, remember you're only a small business owner.

Many people have the wrong idea about life. They wake up in the morning, wash-up, eat, go to work and come home to do it again the next day. That does not have to be your life. Yes, you are living, but can you honestly say that you feel alive? Can you really say to yourself that you can continue to live like this for the rest of your life? Is this the plan you set out for yourself? If you only want to live a <u>simple life</u> you can, but why not live that simple life doing things you love doing? Not doing the things you love doing will stress you out in the long run, meaning it will not bother you now but sooner or later it will!!! I'm a person that dislikes surprises. As I continue to pursue my dreams I realize that life is full of surprises.

Nothing is for sure with business even when it's carefully planned out. Prepare yourself for the worst if that was to happen. I know your probably asking yourself,
"How do I prepare myself for the worst?"

1) You can try getting a <u>short-term</u> investment from two or three <u>family members</u>. Family should not charge you the same interest rate the bank would.
2) You should secure a side job to keep a steady cash flow coming to you.
3) You should not invest more than 25% of your savings, leaving you left with 75% of your savings If anything goes wrong with your small business. With this next

technique you are practically investing everyone's money but your own to start your own business.

I will draw you a graph to show you how this process works. They say that "money don't grow on trees," I agree with that statement 100%. I designed a family tree of 5 family members that would make you think twice about that statement.

FAMILY TREE

	MOM	DAD	BROTHER	SISTER	UNCLE
Jan 1st	$4,000	-1,000	-1,000	-1,000	-1,000
Feb 1st	+3,000	+3,000	-1,000	-1,000	-1,000
March 1st	+2,000	+2,000	+2,000	-1,000	-1,000
April 1st	+1,000	+1,000	+1,000	+1,000	-1,000
May 1st	0	0	0	0	0
June 1st	-1,000	-1,000	-1,000	-1,000	+4,000
July 1st	-1,000	-1,000	-1,000	+3,000	+3,000
August 1st	-1,000	-1,000	+2,000	+2,000	+2,000
Sept 1st	-1,000	+1,000	+1,000	+1,000	+1,000
October 1st	0	0	0	0	0

On January 1st mom will receive $1,000 from dad, brother, sister, and uncle. On February 1st dad will receive $1,000 from mom, brother, sister, and uncle. I know when it finally gets to uncle he have already spent $4,000. Uncle will go again to restart the cycle again giving him a total of $4,000 on June 1st. On July 1st he will have $3,000 because he has to deduct $1,000 to give to his sister. The catch to this family tree is to invest your money wisely while it's in your hand. Everyone should have the chance to go first. There will be no disadvantages, everything should be organized equally. The catch to my technique is to avoid paying interest. You and your family tree members can decide on the amount you want to start with. With a side job and your small business your goal is to maintain your investment. You can have as many members to your family tree as you like. If you decide to have 10 members your goal will be to maintain the $10,000 you will be receiving. So money can grow on trees, a family tree that is☺.

The cycle started with mom and will end with mom. When that happens the rotation will change allowing dad to start the cycle and mom will be at the end of the cycle. When the cycle gets back to dad the rotation will change again, allowing brother to start the cycle placing dad at the end of the cycle. This will continue until everyone has the chance to go first.

Make wise decisions with your investments. Don't risk losing everything knowing that on the next month someone is counting on your payment. This process is only for the ones you trust, that are loyal, responsible and faithful to your <u>family tree</u>. Your family tree doesn't have to consist of real family members. It's only called family tree because once they are in this process they are considered to be family. Families don't lie, cheat, or disrespect one another, that is what my family tree is all about.

My parents have a similar technique they do with their trustworthy friends. On the month of <u>October</u> they will be receiving $2,000 from ten different people giving them a total of $20,000 to invest with. On November they will give only $2,000 out of that $20,000 to the next person in line. This will continue until everyone goes twice. My parents have a different name for this technique, they call it _soul money_. Hard earned money being invested within the family. This technique can also help you catch up with late bill payments, or could be used as extra cash to place a deposit on a house etc, ect. Not just anyone can be able to join this family tree. Someone without any income should not be allowed to join. If something was to happen with the money, where would they get the money to continue making payments? Be extra careful with who you decide to join your family tree, trust is not something that you can easily find.

I once had a friend I thought I could trust. I would have died for this friend, this friend who I trusted like a brother betrayed me. I could have never seen it coming because I had nothing but love and trust for him. My point is that no matter how much you think you know someone never think betrayal is not possible. Whether it is taking something not valuable to lying, is still betrayal no matter how small the situation is. It's really frustrating to me when someone you know all your life betrays you and apologizes after the matter. I always accept their apology but refuse to continue being their friend.

I made honest mistakes in my life, like lying to the woman I love about my name. I only did that because I was wanted for a crime in another country and did not know if it was a wise idea telling her at the time. I did not lie intentionally to hurt you Fadoua and I apologize if I did hurt you, but life has a way of unfolding the truth and the truth is that I was afraid of telling anyone my real name due to my situation with the United States. I believe that one day I will receive her forgiveness, because deep inside her heart she knows I did not mean to hurt her. She has the same attitude I have, it's hard for her to forgive someone that hurt her and that's exactly how I would feel if that was me. As I continue to grow mentally I see that life is too short to hate anyone, when I lost her I started feeling the same way when I lost my cousin or grandfather. Fadoua was a part of me, I guess we were really close, so losing her was like losing a family member.

I did not let this affect my goal, my desire to be successful. To be honest her leaving made me stronger. It must really be true with what they say about "what don't kill you, makes you stronger", because I was down when I lost Fadoua, but now I'm up stronger than ever.

I use to blame everyone but myself for my actions, no one else was responsible for what I did in the past. I'm happy that God gave me a second chance to fix what I can and accept the things I can't change. I love God with every piece of my heart because God kept me strong and alive to fight another day. God understands that I never did anything intentionally to hurt anyone. When you regret and ask forgiveness for the things you have done you are also revealing your sins to God.

Trying to run a business and having enemies makes your job of running a business difficult. How do you expect to achieve your goals constantly thinking about someone hurting you or your business? My advice to you would be to make peace with those that can ruin your business and to treat people the same way you would love to be treated. To be financially successful in this business you need to <u>mind your business</u>. Let me make this a little easier for you to understand. You need to mind what's important for you, your family and your business.

There are many things you can do to make money if you were to take the time working on various ideas you may have thought about. Your ideas may be really good but your <u>time management</u> is poor. If you are struggling financially I advise you to take the opportunity to make a difference before it's gone. Why sit around and imagine being rich? Why prolong your goals if whatever it is your doing is not working for you? I believe that you are afraid of taking chances. If you are having financial problems taking the chances of investing should not be something to think about. You should go ahead and take your chances. What's the worst that can happen if you are already facing a financial crisis? Like I said before in previous chapters, don't wait hoping for a miracle. Don't get me wrong, miracles do exist, they do happen only when you least expect it to. Every good hearted person deserves to live the life they dream of living. It's your life and you can do as you like with it, I'm only trying to encourage you to fight for what you desire.

Not everyone in life is fortunate to be given things on a silver plate, win the lottery or always have nothing but great things happen for them. I always had to fight for what I wanted, struggle to get to my destination or always been told no. The difference with me was that I would not accept anything I was not satisfied with. Your mission in life is to live righteously, satisfy your needs and try helping others achieve their goals. Being helpful to others is really a plus because you never know who you might need in the future. That person you help get their own business may be the next president, best real estate agent or even some big C.E.O at a firm somewhere. Spreading your knowledge to help others can come in handy. How you treat people is how you will be treated as well.

Sometimes you run into really nasty people, people that don't care much for society. Don't allow that to change who you are or want to be. Still, I advise you to try helping that person become a better person, but don't waste too much time trying to help someone that doesn't care for life.

KEY NOTES TO REMEMBER

1) If you're having any doubts about something, don't get involved until you have <u>complete understanding</u> about whatever it is that's bothering you.

2) When it comes to hiring your first employee I advise you to do a background check. It only takes one bad employee to destroy what you had worked so hard for.

3) I urge you to study my family tree graph. This may help you save interest, pay late payments or help you with placing a deposit on a house, car, ect

4) Patch up any misunderstandings you may have with anyone because running a business and having enemies is not an easy task.

5) Be mindful of how hard you had to work and the people who helped you get to where you are. Being successful is a blessing, so help someone else receive the same blessing you have received. Pass your knowledge on to the next person, give them at least a chance.

COMPETITION

As a small business owner know that your success will get the attention of larger companies that would have never paid any attention if your company was not competitive.

Larger companies will find ways to either get involved or try finding ways to better your product making it their own. You should not allow them to think that just because you are a small company you're not keeping updated with the market. You may have the best idea, best product, but was not able to get your message across well. The disadvantage that you will constantly have is not having enough money to simply advertise your company like a larger company would. You will have to work more hours than larger companies because larger companies have paid personnel to handle the hard work. Your budget will also be a problem, you have already planned out your expenses for the year so hiring someone for help would hurt your cash flow. In my previous chapters I spoke about ways to advertise your product. This technique will not harm your budget or affect your cash flow. Read pages (23-24) for ways to advertise your company, stop thinking that you have to spend a lot of money in order to achieve your goals.

Remember, mind your own business!!! What works for someone else may not work for you so think twice before making decisions. If you work according to your standards everything should be a piece of cake. This year I will be competing with myself to lose a certain amount of weight. In order to achieve my goal I must be mentally ready. I'm a person that loves to eat a lot of junk food and fast food. I'm not over weight, but I know that I'm not in top shape. My goal is to work out 5 days a week leaving me with two days off for resting. No matter how hard you work out your body needs rest to heal your muscles. I must cut off any sugar cravings my body ask for and carbohydrates such as bread, rice or pasta. I'm doing this because I want to live a long healthy life, so while I'm competing with myself I will keep in mind how healthy and how sexy my body will be when I'm finish. I should not say finish because this is a process you have to stick with for the rest of your life. What I do want to say is finish with having any cravings.

Mostly everything that you do in life is competitive if you look at it my way. You're competing with other employees for a position at work, competing with other companies, competing in school for better grades to win scholarships and competing when it comes to sports. I can go on and on with this topic but I think you get the point. If you are not living up to your expectations believe that there is always someone else your boss can find to replace you or another company customers can count on. Everyone is replaceable when it comes to working for a company other than your own. How would you handle a customer that is complaining about buying a product from your store that no longer works?

A) Do you first ask for a receipt before taking a look at the customer's merchandise?

B) Do you reject the customer's request for an exchange?

<u>Big Decision:</u>

C) Do you ask for the customers receipt and see if there is a warranty for the merchandise the customer is complaining about?

D) All of the above.

Your decision will make a big difference for your company. I should tell you that satisfying every customer is difficult. Try helping that customer the best way you can so that they will keep coming back believing you have the best service for their money.

If your answer is **(C)** I'm sorry to say you're wrong and you <u>lost business points</u>. Your job is to give your client the best service possible. Asking for a receipt and checking to see if there is any warranty will only upset the customer. You should be simple as possible when it comes to helping a customer, your answer should have been **(A)**. Place yourself in this situation. You just spent money for a flat screen television and after two weeks your television no longer functions. You returned back to the store with your receipt and they are checking to see if you have a warranty for your television. How would you feel as a loyal customer if you were told that no exchanges would be made because you didn't have any warranty? That's my point, It's really heart breaking telling a loyal customer that you will not be able to help them. You will definitely lose a customer and open doors for another company. There will always be doors open for un-satisfied customers. Keep your customers happy, give them the service needed to satisfy their needs and don't give them any attitude. Your customers have been loyal to you for years so it's your job to return the favor.

Maintain your successful business by staying consistent, whatever you had done to get a high demand for your merchandise continue with it. I know you heard the saying <u>"What's not broken don't need fixing"</u>, take this statement serious when it comes to running a successful business. I still advise you to keep a backup plan in case anything does go wrong. Remember, there is nothing wrong with preparing yourself for the future. Your job is to keep your company running, customers satisfied and a steady cash flow. If you still continue to profit from your business after three years from the day you invested you are on your way to financial freedom.

Definition: *Financial Freedom:*

Being able to live your life with no worries about money, having a steady cash flow, money going into your bank account without you building up a sweat and being able to have money continue to grow without having to go to work. Once you get to this level taking chances on different aspects of business should not hurt you if things were to go wrong. One of my goals is to have financial freedom, if I work according to my plans I will achieve this goal. There is a big difference from someone being rich and someone having financial freedom.

A millionaire is rich, but a millionaire may not have financial freedom. A millionaire may have to continue working to maintain his/her millions, example: A professional basketball player just received a 5 million dollar contract. After 2 years of playing was cut off the team for lack of performance. Playing basketball was the only sort of income. The professional basketball player never thought about investing, believing that 5 million dollars would last forever. Now someone with hundreds of property has a cash flow of 60 thousand a month can live comfortable not having to worry about where his/her money will come from to pay their bills. They don't have to worry about getting fired whatsoever. They have it to a point where there money is <u>working for them!!!</u>, so under what category would you want to live your life? Do you rather have a million dollars with no investments or cash flow? Do you rather have small investments and a steady cash flow which would make you a millionaire eventually?

If you are actually thinking about which one you prefer having your not ready to invest or take on responsibility. What would you profit from having a million dollars with no idea about what to invest on? With no plans or investments the only strategy you will have is being able to spend it all. I do know that the economy is falling apart, but like I said on my previous chapters to try using your mind instead of your eyes. Being a successful business men/women is very competitive. Nothing will be given to you without hard work, the only thing that is promising is getting old and death!!! So why not make your life as comfortable as possible so that when you do get old you will be already establish?

It may not be a bad idea to start off small so that you will have a better understanding how investments work. I guarantee that you will be more comfortable after profiting from your first deal. You will know and understand how to attack the market. There is nothing wrong with taking baby steps to improve your business skills. If your business fails don't blame yourself entirely, the location of where your business is placed plays a major part. Allow customers to be accustomed to your place of business. Set flyers, magazine ads, ect. Placing your company near a larger successful business will not help you at all. Research the area well before thinking about placing your business in that location.

KEY POINTS TO REMEMBER

1) Make sure to stay updated with the market.

2) Keep your budget simple as possible, anything extra may hurt you financially.

3) Try treating your customers with the best service possible. Your customers play a major part with your success.

4) If everything seems to be running well stay with it, stay consistent and remember that if nothing is broken don't try fixing it.

I hope that from reading my book you will find the confidence, motivation and knowledge to not only chase your dreams but achieve them as well. Follow my steps and my techniques on your journey to success. Believe in yourself because if you don't no one will believe in you and that will lead to failure.

I wanted to succeed because I was tired of going to prison, tired of always failing from doing the wrong things and tired of hurting my family. I realized when you constantly procrastinate with something not only will you make that a habit, you will not be taken serious when it comes to making business agreements. I strive for success, for financial freedom, for pure healthy love, love that does not hurt, love that makes you feel joyful and love that will be by your side when times are <u>good</u> or <u>bad</u>.

It was really hard for me to do things I wanted to because I was always too busy doing things for others. Being helpful is never a bad thing but try helping yourself first, try doing the things you love doing, try living your life before thinking about helping someone live theirs. Take my advice with you, take my encouragement, my direction to find your way. It's time for you to be your own boss, make your own decisions and be a good example for leadership. I know you will succeed because you got this far, you took the time to read my book. From this day on, I believe you will make a difference in today's society, I believe you will not give up without a fight. I thank you for trying to make a change in your life. If there is anything that would make me feel good, it would be to see the world we live in not struggle to make ends meet.

DEDICATIONS

Christian and Lucie Jean-Louis, the best parents God have given to me. I thank them for never giving up on me, for loving me, for believing that I would make a difference, a positive change and for lifting up my spirit.

I want to give thanks to Reginald Herrisse, Henry Claude Laflanc, Dominic Laflanc, Castro Camay and Wesler for their un-conditional love. Wesler was taken away from us due to a violent crime but I know he is in heaven looking down on me with a smile on his face. Thank you, Wesler for always being supportive. I respect these men, there true friends because they never looked down at me as a criminal or stranger when I was exposed of my true identity and when I went to prison.

I want to thank <u>Fadoua</u> for her honesty, loyalty and for never misleading me. Thank you Fadoua for pushing me towards success and thank you for encouraging me to fight for what I believe in. I'm sorry if I hurt you, sorry if I ever mislead you into thinking I was who I said I was. It was not my intentions to hurt anyone, I was afraid. If you know me, you know that I'm a respectful and loving person. What happened in the past should be left in the past, so don't allow that to determine my character. I only hope that you give me a chance to make up the lost time we missed due to my imprisonment.

$ Profit $ 101 volume 1
Test

1) <u>What will you achieve by running from your problems?</u>
   A) winning
   B) not having to deal with it
   C) losing, getting into more problems and you will not learn anything by avoiding them
   D) All of the above

2) <u>What is the secret of *money*?</u>
   A) spend more than you make
   B) working hard to save your money
   C) investing to a point where money is working for you
   D) make money to pay bills on time

3) <u>If I won a million dollars would I be stress free financially?</u>
   A) Yes
   B) No

4) <u>Is a professional athlete stress free financially after retirement with no future investments or cash flow?</u>
   A) Yes
   B) No

5) <u>What do you consider to be an asset?</u>
   A) Investment property
   B) my home
   C) my car
   D) All of the above

6) <u>What is an example of liability?</u>
   A) money constantly coming out my pocket
   B) paying mortgage on your home
   C) my nice car
   D) All of the above

7) <u>What category do banks look at someone with bad credit and no cash flow?</u>
   A) Liability
   B) Risk
   C) Poor class
   D) All of the above

8) <u>What are my six enemies in the world of business?</u>

   1)   3)   6)

   2)   4)   7)

9) <u>What is an example of *Financial Freedom*?</u>
    A) working to make money
    B) having a steady cash flow/money constantly going into your pockets
    C) to have a million dollars/no investment
    D) All of the above

10) <u>What is an example of cash flow?</u>
    A) steady income every month from other people paying you
    B) working for someone else for money
    C) depositing money in your checking/ savings account every month
    D) All of the above

$ Profit $ 101 volume 1
Answer Key

"If you are looking at this answer key before trying to answer the questions on your own, you are cheating, and you did not understand what my book is about. Taking shortcuts rather than testing your knowledge is pointless. What will you learn by always taking shortcuts?"

1) C
2) C
3) B
4) B
5) A
6) D
7) D
8) I can't, no, never, tired, stupid, lazy
9) B
10) A